Start TO Finish
Second Series

FROM River TO Raindrop

THE WATER CYCLE

EMMA CARLSON BERNE

LERNER PUBLICATIONS · Minneapolis

Lerner Publications Company
A division of Lerner Publishing Group, Inc.
241 First Avenue North
Minneapolis, MN 55401 USA

For reading levels and more information, look up this title at www.lernerbooks.com.

Library of Congress Cataloging-in-Publication Data

Names: Berne, Emma Carlson, author.
Title: From river to raindrop : the water cycle / Emma Carlson Berne.
Other titles: Start to finish (Minneapolis, Minn.). Second series.
Description: Minneapolis : Lerner Publications, [2018] | Series: Start to finish. Second series | Audience: Ages 5-9. | Audience: K to grade 3. | Includes bibliographical references and index.
Identifiers: LCCN 2016037262 (print) | LCCN 2016042643 (ebook) | ISBN 9781512434422 (lb : alk. paper) | ISBN 9781512450941 (eb pdf)
Subjects: LCSH: Hydrologic cycle—Juvenile literature. | Rain and rainfall—Juvenile literature.
Classification: LCC GB848 .B4685 2018 (print) | LCC GB848 (ebook) | DDC 551.48—dc23

LC record available at https://lccn.loc.gov/2016037262

Manufactured in the United States of America
1-42091-25385-9/27/2016

TABLE OF **Contents**

Rain taps my umbrella. Where does it come from?

Water runs through rivers and streams.

The water flows beneath the sky, clouds, and sun. The sun shines down on the water. It warms the water's surface.

Drops on the water's surface evaporate.

Warmth from the sun causes the evaporation.
Evaporation is when water turns into a gas.
The water drops turn into a gas called water vapor.

The evaporated drops float on the wind.

The wind carries the water vapor up into the sky. It sails toward the clouds and sun. Soon it is high above Earth.

The drops become part of a cloud.

The water vapor joins with a cloud in the sky. The water vapor cools off when it joins with a cloud. It is much cooler now than it was when it first formed.

The drops turn back into a liquid.

When it gets cool enough, water vapor turns back into a liquid. The water vapor is now in the same form as it was when it started out as drops from a river. This is called condensation.

The drops in the cloud stick to bits of dust.

Clouds have tiny bits of dust in them. There is also wind inside a cloud. The wind mixes the dust and water drops together. This creates **droplets** of rain.

The droplets swirl and gather water.

The droplets grow bigger and bigger. They also get heavier and heavier. The water they pick up inside the cloud gives them lots of weight.

The heavy droplets fall from the cloud.

When the droplets are heavy enough, they fall as rain. They make puddles you can splash in!

The rain brings water to Earth.

The rain helps plants grow. It gives animals water to drink. It falls into rivers and streams. Then the water cycle begins again.

Glossary

condensation: when gas cools and becomes a liquid

droplets: very small drops of liquid

evaporate: to change from a liquid into a gas

gas: a substance that is like air and has no fixed shape

liquid: a substance that flows freely and is not a solid or a gas

water vapor: liquid water that has turned into a gas

Further Information

Duke, Shirley. *Step-by-Step Experiments with the Water Cycle*. Mankato, MN: Child's World, 2012. Explore the water cycle through fun, hands-on experiments.

Enchanted Learning: The Water Cycle
http://www.enchantedlearning.com/subjects/astronomy/planets/earth/Watercycle.shtml
See a water cycle diagram and read more about the cycle at this website.

Higgins, Nadia. *Discover Water*. Mankato, MN: Child's World, 2014. This easy-to-read book discusses the three forms of water: liquid, solid, and gas.

Ransom, Candice. *Investigating the Water Cycle*. Minneapolis: Lerner Publications, 2016. Take a detailed look at the water cycle with this book.

USGS: The Water Cycle
http://water.usgs.gov/edu/watercycle-kids-adv.html
Readers interested in deeper exploration will enjoy this interactive water cycle diagram.

Index

Photo Acknowledgments

The images in this book are used with the permission of: © Jon Bilous/Shutterstock.com, p. 1; © iStockphoto.com/PeopleImages, p. 3; © iStockphoto.com/Mihai Andritoiu, p. 5; © iStockphoto.com/OlenaMykhaylova, p. 7; © iStockphoto.com/Silent_GOS, p. 9; © Vibrant Image Studio/Shutterstock.com, p. 11; © iStockphoto.com/Cindy Singleton, p. 13; © Cleo/Dreamstime.com, p. 15; © iStockphoto.com/emholk, p. 19; © blickwinkel/S Gerth/Alamy, p. 21.

Cover: © iStockphoto.com/naumoid.

Main body text set in Arta Std Book 20/26.
Typeface provided by International Typeface Corp.

LERNER
e
SOURCE™

Expand learning beyond the printed book. Download free, complementary educational resources for this book from our website, www.lerneresource.com.